Patrick McDonald

Potato Dishes

PATRICK MCDONALD

Potato Dishes

Photography by Simon Wheeler

WEIDENFELD & NICOLSON

Patrick McDonald

Patrick McDonald was born in Northumberland, the son of a farmer and estate keeper. Patrick discovered his passion for food at an early age, while watching his mother and grandmother cook with the fresh ingredients his father brought in from the land.

He trained under Anton Mosimann at the Dorchester Hotel, and later became head chef of the Manor House Hotel in Wiltshire.

His first restaurant, The Epicurean in Cheltenham, Gloucestershire, won a plethora of stars, rosettes and rave reviews in the national press for his varied, innovative and distinctive style of cooking. In 1995 he joined Harvey Nichols as consultant chef.

Patrick McDonald is now consultant chef and restaurant adviser for Sir Rocco Forte Hotels, and a partner in Les Saveurs restaurant in London. He is married and has three children.

Contents

THE BASICS

Let the sky rain potatoes.

WILLIAM SHAKESPEARE
(1564–1616)

Introduction

Brought to Europe by the Spanish from their travels in South America, the potato soon became one of the major food sources in the British Isles. Potatoes are very good for us, providing vitamin C, carbohydrate, fibre and some minerals and proteins. Of course, if they are served with lashings of butter or cream they will pile on the pounds and the inches, but plain boiled, steamed or baked potatoes are low in calories. However, I am not a dietician, I am a cook who is passionate about food. The recipes I have chosen for this book are based upon simple ideas, yet they can easily achieve gourmet status. Some are classics and others are long-standing favourites from my restaurants.

I have selected a specific potato for each recipe, but this doesn't mean the dish will not work unless that variety is used, it refers only to my personal choice. Try these recipes and create something stunning out of something so simple ... the potato.

BAKED NEW POTATOES
with smoked salmon, crème fraîche and caviar

SERVES 4

12 Jersey Royal or Roseval
    potatoes
225 g/8 oz sea salt
85 g/3 oz smoked salmon,
    cut into fine strips
85 g/3 oz crème fraîche
juice of ½ lemon
small bunch of chives, finely
    chopped
salt and pepper
85 g/3 oz caviar (optional)
sprigs of chervil

Preheat the oven to 200°C/400°F/Gas Mark 6.

Prick each potato two or three times with a fork, then wrap in foil. Spread the sea salt in an ovenproof dish, which should be just large enough to hold the potatoes in a single layer. Sit the wrapped potatoes on the salt, place in the oven and bake for about 45–55 minutes or until cooked through.

In a bowl, mix together the smoked salmon, crème fraîche, lemon juice and chives. Season to taste.

When the potatoes are cooked, remove from the dish and cut a cross in the top of each one. Mix the sea salt with 2–3 tablespoons water and divide this between four plates, as a base for the potatoes. Open up the potatoes and spoon in the smoked salmon mixture. Serve at once, topped with caviar and a sprig of chervil.

Serve as a starter or perhaps a light supper dish, followed by roast chicken with lemon and rosemary.

LEEK AND POTATO SOUP
scented with basil

SERVES 4

125 g/4 oz butter
400 g/14 oz leeks, chopped
225 g/8 oz onions, chopped
325 g/12 oz Maris Piper
    potatoes, chopped
1.2 litres/2 pints chicken stock
250 ml/8 fl oz double cream
12 fresh basil leaves
salt and pepper

Melt the butter in a deep, heavy-bottomed saucepan, add the leeks and onions and cook over a low heat until soft but not browned. Add the potatoes and stock and simmer until the potatoes are soft and tender.

Add the cream and simmer for a further 5 minutes. Add the basil leaves and purée in a liquidizer or food processor. Pass through a sieve and season to taste. To serve, reheat gently.

A perfect, simple starter on its own, or serve with tomato crostini to make a more wholesome meal. Follow with calves' liver with braised celery, then mango tarte tatin with vanilla ice cream.

THAI SPICED CRAB AND POTATO CROQUETTES

SERVES 4

450 g/1 lb Desiree potatoes,
    very finely diced
50 g/2 oz butter
85 g/3 oz shallots, sliced
2 garlic cloves, crushed
4 eggs
2 tablespoons soy sauce
2 tablespoons Thai fish sauce
small bunch of coriander,
    chopped
½ teaspoon grated fresh ginger
juice of 2 limes
1–3 tablespoons sweet chilli
    sauce
salt and pepper
225 g/8 oz fresh white crabmeat
50 ml/2 fl oz milk
125 g/4 oz Japanese or dried
    breadcrumbs
85 g/3 oz plain flour
vegetable oil for deep-frying

Place the diced potatoes in a saucepan of cold salted water, bring to the boil, then turn down the heat and simmer until tender. Drain and return to the warm pan to dry thoroughly.

Meanwhile, melt the butter in a saucepan, add the shallots and garlic and cook over a low heat until soft but not browned.

Put the potatoes in a large bowl. Beat two of the eggs and add to the bowl, with the shallots and garlic, soy sauce, fish sauce, coriander, ginger, lime juice, chilli sauce and seasonng to taste. Mix together well, then add the crabmeat and mix in lightly but evenly. Chill in the refrigerator for 3–4 hours.

Beat the remaining eggs and milk together in a bowl and spread the breadcrumbs on a plate. Divide the potato mixture into twelve croquettes and coat each in flour. Dip the croquettes into the egg mixture to coat evenly, then coat in the breadcrumbs.

Heat the oil for deep-frying to 180–190°C/350–375°F or until a cube of bread browns in 30 seconds. Fry the croquettes until golden brown, drain on paper towels and serve hot, with a spicy tomato salsa.

Continue the Thai theme with a main course of salmon with coconut noodles, lemongrass and lime leaves, and a dessert of poached lychees.

Black pudding and champ, shallots and red wine sauce

SERVES 4

325 g/12 oz Pentland Hawk
    potatoes, chopped
325 g/12 oz black pudding
2 tablespoons olive oil
85 g/3 oz butter
2 bunches of spring onions,
    finely chopped
4 tablespoons double cream
salt and pepper

Glazed shallots
16–20 shallots or button onions
85 g/3 oz butter
50 g/2 oz caster sugar
2 sprigs of thyme

To serve
Red wine sauce (page 34)

For the glazed shallots, put the shallots in a saucepan of cold water, bring to the boil for about 1 minute, then drain. Melt the butter and sugar in a frying pan, add the shallots, a splash of water and the thyme. Cover the shallots with a butter paper or foil and cook over a low heat until all the liquid has evaporated and the shallots are tender.

Meanwhile, place the potatoes in a saucepan of cold salted water, bring to the boil, then turn down the heat and simmer until tender. Drain and mash.

Slice the black pudding into small discs, then fry lightly in the olive oil.

The shallots should by now be coated in a light caramelized glaze. If they are not, turn up the heat and gently roll the shallots around the pan. Season to taste.

Melt the butter in a large saucepan, add the spring onions and cook for just long enough to soften them, then add the mashed potato and cream and beat well. To serve, spoon the champ on to four plates, scatter the glazed shallots around and lay the black pudding on top. Finally, pour over the red wine sauce.

All you need by way of accompaniment is a large plate of Irish oysters and a pint of Guinness.

POTATO AND FOIE GRAS MILLE FEUILLES

SERVES 4

25 g/1 oz butter
2 tablespoons olive oil
175 g/6 oz shallots, sliced
1 teaspoon red wine vinegar
325 g/12 oz Maris Piper
    potatoes, finely grated
salt and pepper
4 tablespoons vegetable oil
400 g/14 oz fresh foie gras or
    chicken livers
225 g/8 oz mixed lettuce leaves
15 g/½ oz fresh black truffle,
    sliced (optional)
4–6 tablespoons Garlic cream
    dressing (page 36)

Heat the butter and olive oil in a frying pan, add the shallots and cook until soft and browned. Add the vinegar and cook for a further 5 minutes.

Season the grated potatoes with salt and pepper. Place a 10 cm/4 inch diameter metal pastry cutter in a large frying pan. Heat the pan and trickle a little of the vegetable oil into the pastry cutter. Add some of the grated potato, to form a very thin layer. When the potato begins to colour, turn it over and cook lightly on the other side until crisp. Repeat this process to make 12 potato layers.

Slice the foie gras into eight pieces and sauté quickly over a high heat. Season lightly and remove from the pan.

To assemble the dish, place a potato layer on each plate, top with a teaspoon of shallots and then a piece of foie gras. Repeat, then top with a final layer of potato. Surround with lettuce leaves and truffle slices, then drizzle over the dressing.

A decadent starter to precede any dish, from a simple piece of seared salmon fillet to roast pigeon (ideally from Bresse) with fresh ceps.

TERRINE OF POTATO, CABBAGE AND PORK KNUCKLE, SAUCE GRIBICHE

SERVES 12

4 ham hocks
8 carrots, chopped
6 onions, chopped
6 leeks, chopped
4 sticks of celery, chopped
4 bay leaves
1 whole bulb of garlic, split in
   half
2.3 litres/4 pints chicken stock
3 sheets of leaf gelatine, soaked
325 g/12 oz savoy cabbage,
   shredded
85 g/3 oz butter
12 sage leaves, chopped
salt and pepper
4 large Estima potatoes, cubed
300 ml/½ pint milk

To serve
Sauce gribiche (page 35)
sprigs of herbs

Place the hocks in a large saucepan with the carrots, onions, leeks, celery, bay leaves, garlic and chicken stock. Top up with water and bring to the boil, skim off any impurities, then cover and simmer gently for 3 hours.

Remove the hocks from the cooking liquid and leave to cool, then remove the cooked meat from the bone and cut into chunks. Pass the liquid through a fine sieve two or three times, then return to a clean pan and boil to reduce to 600 ml/1 pint. Stir in the gelatine until dissolved.

Blanch the cabbage in boiling water, drain and refresh in cold running water. Melt the butter in a saucepan with the sage, add the cabbage and finish cooking in the butter. Season to taste.

Put the potatoes in a saucepan with the milk and a little salt and pepper. Simmer until tender. Drain well.

To assemble, line a long, rectangular terrine with a double layer of cling film, leaving a generous amount hanging over each side. Fill the terrine with layers of ham, cabbage and potato, moistening each layer with the reduced cooking liquid until the terrine is filled. Wrap the terrine with the overhanging cling film and lay a weight on top, then refrigerate for 48 hours.

To serve, turn out the terrine and slice (still in the cling film). Lay each slice on a plate, then remove the cling film. Serve with sauce gribiche and garnish with herbs.

This dish takes a little time to prepare, but it's great for a buffet dish or starter for a large dinner party. Follow with pan-fried turbot with chive butter sauce, or roast duck.

IRISH STEW

SERVES 4

8 lamb chops
25 g/1 oz lamb fat
25 g/1 oz butter
175 g/6 oz onions, sliced
175 g/6 oz carrots, sliced
125 g/4 oz leeks, sliced
2 garlic cloves, chopped
1 bay leaf
2 sprigs of rosemary
125 g/4 oz pearl barley
400–450 g/14–16 oz Wilja
   potatoes, cut into large dice
1.2 litres/2 pints chicken stock
salt and pepper
175 g/6 oz cabbage, shredded
25 g/1 oz flat-leaf parsley,
   chopped

Blanch the chops in a pan of boiling water, then remove and refresh in cold water.

Melt the butter and lamb fat in a casserole, add the onions, carrots, leeks and garlic and cook over a low heat until softened. Add the chops, bay leaf, rosemary, pearl barley and potatoes, then add the chicken stock and about 600 ml/1 pint water to cover. Bring to the boil, skim off any impurities, then cover and simmer for 35–40 minutes or until the meat is tender.

To serve, add the cabbage to the casserole and cook for a further 4–5 minutes. Add the chopped parsley and season with salt and pepper. Serve in deep bowls, pouring the cooking liquid over the meat and vegetables.

Serve a dish of buttered green beans to accompany the stew. When my grandmother made Irish stew it was always followed by a steamed pudding, usually spotted dick.

CORNED BEEF HASH

SERVES 4

450–500 g/16–18 oz Pentland
   Dell potatoes, quartered
125 g/4 oz butter
225 g/8 oz onions, sliced
125 g/4 oz leeks, roughly
   chopped
2 x 400 g/14 oz tins of corned
   beef, diced
8 tablespoons Worcestershire
   sauce
25 g/1 oz flat-leaf parsley,
   chopped
salt and pepper

To serve
4 eggs, poached
Hollandaise sauce (page 35)

Boil the potatoes in salted water until tender. Melt the butter in a frying pan, add the onions and leeks and cook over a low heat until soft but not browned.

When the potatoes are cooked, drain and add to the onions and leeks. Add the diced corned beef, Worcestershire sauce, parsley and seasoning to taste, and mix together.

Divide the hash between four plates, top each with a poached egg and coat with Hollandaise sauce.

Comfort food at its best, great for breakfast, lunch or supper.

POTATO DUMPLINGS
with wilted spinach and Parmesan

SERVES 4

900 g/2 lb Catriona potatoes
3 egg yolks
150 g/5 oz plain flour
salt and pepper
250 ml/8 fl oz double cream
225 g/8 oz baby leaf spinach
175 g/6 oz fresh Parmesan
    cheese, grated

Preheat the oven to 200°C/400°F/Gas Mark 6.

Bake the potatoes in their skins until the flesh is soft and tender, about 1–1½ hours.

Scoop out the potato flesh into a bowl and mash while still hot. Add the egg yolks and flour, season to taste and beat to a smooth dough. Divide the mixture into 2.5 cm/1 inch diameter balls and lay on a floured tray. Chill until ready to cook.

Bring a wide saucepan of water to the boil, add salt and reduce the heat to a gentle simmer. Lower in the dumplings and simmer for 8–12 minutes. Test one to check that they are cooked through, then drain and place in a serving dish. Preheat the grill.

Pour the cream into a saucepan and boil to reduce by half. Add the spinach and half the Parmesan. Heat through for 2 minutes, just long enough to wilt the spinach, then pour over the dumplings and sprinkle with the remaining Parmesan. Place under the hot grill for 3 minutes, until golden and bubbling. Serve hot.

As this is an Italian-influenced dish, start with tomato and basil bruschetta. After the dumplings, finish with pannacotta or zabaglione and biscotti. Don't forget the Pinot Grigio.

BREAST OF DUCK
with dauphinoise potatoes and Madeira sauce

SERVES 4

125 g/4 oz butter
450 g/1 lb Cara potatoes,
    sliced into thin discs
4 garlic cloves, crushed
4 pinches of freshly grated
    nutmeg
salt and pepper
300 ml/½ pint double cream
300 ml/½ pint milk
4 duck breasts, about 175–
    200 g/6–7 oz each

To serve
Madeira sauce (page 34)
roasted shallots (page 37)

Preheat the oven to 200°C/400°F/Gas Mark 6.

Melt the butter in a large deep saucepan over a low heat. Add the potatoes, garlic, nutmeg, salt and pepper. Cook over a low heat for 3–5 minutes, stirring frequently, then add the cream and milk and simmer gently for 7–8 minutes. Transfer to an ovenproof dish and place in the oven for 25 minutes or until golden brown on top. Leave to rest for 10–15 minutes.

Season the duck breasts with salt and pepper. Place the breasts skin side down in a cold frying pan and bring up to a high heat; this will allow a lot of the fat to be released from the skin. Turn over and cook until sealed and golden. Transfer the breasts to a baking sheet and place in the oven for 6 minutes. Remove from the oven and leave to rest.

To serve, slice the duck breasts on to four dinner plates. Serve with some dauphinoise potatoes (if you like, you can use a round pastry cutter to cut out small gateaux of potato) and roasted shallots and pour the sauce over.

Serve as a dinner party main course with buttered carrots and asparagus (pages 36 and 37). Alternatively, the dauphinoise potatoes topped with cheese and bacon make a meal in themselves.

COD FILLET WRAPPED IN POTATO
with bacon, onions and red wine sauce

SERVES 4

4 pieces of cod fillet, about
   175–200 g/ 6–7 oz each
salt and pepper
4 large Maris Piper potatoes,
   peeled
200 g/7 oz butter
225 g/8 oz pancetta bacon,
   cut into lardons
175 g/6 oz button onions
50 g/2 oz caster sugar
2 sprigs of thyme

To serve
Red wine sauce (page 34)

Season the cod and chill in the refrigerator.

Grate the potatoes very finely, then squeeze out any excess liquid in a tea towel. Melt half the butter and brush the chilled cod with melted butter. Press the grated potato on to the fish, applying more butter as you add the potato until each fillet is totally encased in potato. Wrap tightly in cling film and chill in the refrigerator for 1 hour.

Put the button onions in a saucepan of cold water, bring to the boil for about 1 minute, then drain. Melt the remaining butter and sugar in a frying pan, add the onions, a splash of water and the thyme. Cover with a butter paper or foil and cook over a low heat until the liquid has evaporated and the onions are tender.

Preheat the oven to 200°C/400°F/Gas Mark 6.

Heat a little butter in a large frying pan, add the bacon and the fish and cook until the potato is lightly coloured all over. Place in the oven and bake for 8–10 minutes or until the potato is golden brown.

The button onions should be coated in a light caramelized glaze. If they are not, turn up the heat and gently roll them around the pan. Season to taste.

To serve, heat the red wine sauce. Place a piece of potato-wrapped fish in the centre of each plate, pour the sauce around and garnish with the bacon and button onions.

Serve with buttered leaf spinach. Begin the meal with a starter of duck confit or terrine and finish with pear soufflé.

SALAD OF NEW POTATOES, LOBSTER AND TRUFFLES

SERVES 4

450 g/1 lb Belle de Fontenay
    potatoes, scraped
125 g/4 oz butter
1 shallot, finely chopped
85 ml/3 fl oz olive oil
2 tablespoons white wine vinegar
salt and pepper
4 lobsters, cooked, about
    450g/1 lb each
1 bunch of chives
1 bunch of chervil
1 black truffle
2 tablespoons white truffle oil

Put the potatoes in a saucepan with the butter and just enough water to cover. Bring to the boil and simmer until tender. Cut each potato in half lengthways and place in a bowl. Add the shallot, olive oil, vinegar, 2 tablespoons water and salt and pepper. Turn the potatoes in the liquid and leave to stand for 8–10 minutes.

Remove the lobster flesh from the shells and cut into even slices.

Lay the warm potatoes on four plates, arrange the lobster on top of the potatoes and spoon over some of the oil and vinegar dressing. Garnish with chives, chervil and slices of truffle, and finally drizzle over the truffle oil.

To make this into a complete meal, serve with a bowl of salad leaves and follow with a simple slice of lemon tart.

The Basics

MADEIRA SAUCE

SERVES 4

2 tablespoons olive oil
175 g/6 oz meat, diced (whichever
    meat the sauce is to
    accompany)
4 shallots, sliced
12 button mushrooms, sliced
4 garlic cloves, sliced
2 sprigs of thyme
1 small bay leaf
6 black peppercorns, coarsely
    crushed
1 tablespoon red wine vinegar
300 ml/10 fl oz Madeira
300 ml/10 fl oz veal stock
300 ml/10 fl oz chicken stock

Heat half the oil in a saucepan, add the meat and cook over high heat until the meat is sealed and golden brown, turning frequently.

Heat the remaining oil in a frying pan over a moderate to high heat, add the shallots, mushrooms, garlic, thyme, bay leaf and peppercorns and sauté until lightly browned. Add the vinegar and boil until all the moisture has evaporated.

Add the shallot mixture to the meat, pour over the Madeira and boil to reduce by half.

Add the stocks and bring to the boil, then skim and reduce the heat. Simmer for 30–40 minutes.

Remove from the heat and leave to stand for 5 minutes. Strain several times through a muslin-lined sieve to remove impurities and make a wonderful clear sauce.

RED WINE SAUCE

SERVES 4
1 tablespoon olive oil
2 shallots, finely sliced
1–2 bottles red wine
175 ml/6 fl oz ruby port
600 ml/1 pint veal stock
85 g/3 oz unsalted butter, diced
salt and pepper

Heat the oil in a saucepan, add the shallots and cook over a low heat until soft but not browned.

Add the red wine and port and boil to reduce by three-quarters. Add the stock and boil to reduce to about 200 ml/7 fl oz.

Add the butter and whisk vigorously. Season to taste.

Sauce gribiche

SERVES 12

6 hard-boiled eggs
175 g/6 oz gherkins
175 g/6 oz capers
1 bunch of tarragon,
   finely chopped
1 bunch of parsley,
   finely chopped
4 tablespoons olive oil
salt and pepper

Separate the egg yolks from the whites and chop each very finely or push through a sieve.

Chop the gherkins and capers together very finely and mix together with the egg yolk and white. Add the herbs and oil, mix together, and season to taste.

Hollandaise sauce

SERVES 4

225 g/8 oz butter
4 egg yolks
juice of ½ lemon
salt
cayenne pepper

Melt the butter in a small saucepan (preferably one with a pouring lip).

Put the egg yolks and 4 teaspoons water into a mixing bowl and whisk until the yolks become almost white in colour and are very light and foamy.

Place the bowl over a pan of simmering (not boiling) water and continue to whisk vigorously while you gently pour in the melted butter, a little at a time, in a thin stream. When the sauce is creamy, stop whisking and beat in the lemon juice, salt and cayenne pepper to taste.

GARLIC CREAM DRESSING

MAKES 600 ML/1 PINT

2 teaspoons brown sugar
3 teaspoons Dijon mustard
6 garlic cloves, crushed
85 ml/3 fl oz sherry vinegar
200 ml/7 fl oz olive oil
200 ml/7 fl oz peanut oil
85 ml/3 fl oz double cream
salt and pepper

Put the sugar, mustard, garlic and vinegar in a mixing bowl and mix well until the sugar has dissolved.

While beating vigorously, gently pour in the oils a little at a time until fully incorporated and emulsified. Finally whisk in the cream and beat well until smooth. Season to taste.

BUTTERED ASPARAGUS

SERVES 4

48 asparagus stalks
125 g/4 oz butter
salt and pepper

Peel the asparagus from 5 cm/2 inches below the tip to the base of each stalk. Blanch the asparagus in boiling salted water for 1–2 minutes, then drain and refresh under cold running water.

To finish the asparagus, put the butter in a saucepan with about 4 tablespoons water and bring to the boil; this will form an emulsion. Reheat the asparagus in the emulsion, season to taste and serve at once.

Glazed baby carrots

SERVES 4

1 bunch of baby carrots
   (about 16–20 carrots)
85 g/3 oz butter
1 tablespoon caster sugar
salt

Wash the carrots well, rubbing the skins gently or peeling very finely. Cut off the tops, leaving about 2.5 cm/1 inch of green. Cook the carrots in boiling salted water until just tender, then drain and refresh under cold running water.

To glaze, put the butter and sugar in a deep frying pan and heat until bubbling. Add the carrots and roll them around until they are coated in a shiny glaze.

Roasted shallots

SERVES 4

12–16 shallots
sea salt
125 ml/4 fl oz olive oil
4 sprigs of rosemary
4 bay leaves

Preheat the oven to 200°C/400°F/Gas Mark 6. Trim the roots off the shallots.

Cover the base of an ovenproof dish with sea salt to form a 1 cm/½ inch deep bed.

Cut out two squares of foil measuring about 30 x 30 cm/12 x 12 inches. Crimp three edges together to make a pouch. Put the shallots in the pouch, add the oil and herbs, then crimp the final edge to seal.

Place on the bed of salt and cook in the oven for 1–2 hours or until tender. Serve the shallots in their skins, with a little of the cooking juices brushed over.

Classic Cooking

STARTERS

Jean Christophe Novelli Chef/patron of Maison Novelli, which opened in London to great acclaim in 1996. He previously worked at the Four Seasons restaurant, London.

VEGETABLE SOUPS

Elisabeth Luard Cookery writer for the *Sunday Telegraph Magazine* and author of *European Peasant Food* and *European Festival Food*, which won a Glenfiddich Award.

GOURMET SALADS

Sonia Stevenson The first woman chef in the UK to be awarded a Michelin star, at the Horn of Plenty in Devon. Author of *The Magic of Saucery* and *Fresh Ways with Fish*.

FISH AND SHELLFISH

Gordon Ramsay Chef/proprietor of one of London's most popular restaurants, Aubergine, recently awarded its second Michelin star. He is the author of *A Passion for Flavour*.

CHICKEN, DUCK AND GAME

Nick Nairn Chef/patron of Braeval restaurant near Aberfoyle in Scotland, whose BBC-TV series *Wild Harvest* was last summer's most successful cookery series, accompanied by a book.

LIVERS, SWEETBREADS AND KIDNEYS

Simon Hopkinson Former chef/patron at London's Bibendum restaurant, columnist and author of *Roast Chicken and Other Stories* and the forthcoming *The Prawn Cocktail Years*.

VEGETARIAN

Rosamond Richardson Author of several vegetarian titles, including *The Great Green Gourmet* and *Food from Green Places*. She has also appeared on television.

PASTA

Joy Davies One of the creators of *BBC Good Food Magazine*, she has been food editor of *She, Woman* and *Options* and written for the *Guardian, Daily Telegraph* and *Harpers & Queen*.

CHEESE DISHES

Rose Elliot The UK's most successful vegetarian cookery writer and author of many books, including *Not Just a Load of Old Lentils* and *The Classic Vegetarian Cookbook*.

POTATO DISHES

Patrick McDonald Author of the forthcoming *Simply Good Food* and Harvey Nichols' food consultant.

BISTRO COOKING

Anne Willan Founder and director of La Varenne Cookery School in Burgundy and West Virginia. Author of many books and a specialist in French cuisine.

ITALIAN COOKING

Anna Del Conte is the author of *The Classic Food of Northern Italy* (chosen as the 1996 Guild of Food Writers Book of the Year) and *The Gastronomy of Italy*. She has appeared on BBC-TV's *Masterchef*.

VIETNAMESE COOKING
Nicole Routhier One of the United States' most popular cookery writers, her books include *Cooking Under Wraps*, *Nicole Routhier's Fruit Cookbook* and the award-winning *The Foods of Vietnam*.

MALAYSIAN COOKING
Jill Dupleix One of Australia's best known cookery writers, with columns in the *Sydney Morning Herald* and *Elle*. Author of *New Food*, *Allegro al dente* and the Master Chefs *Pacific*.

PEKING CUISINE
Helen Chen Learned to cook traditional Peking dishes from her mother, Joyce Chen, the grande dame of Chinese cooking in the United States. The author of *Chinese Home Cooking*.

STIR FRIES
Kay Fairfax Author of several books, including *100 Great Stir-fries*, *Homemade* and *The Australian Christmas Book*.

NOODLES
Terry Durack Australia's most widely read restaurant critic and co-editor of the *Sydney Morning Herald Good Food Guide*. He is the author of *YUM!*, a book of stories and recipes.

NORTH INDIAN CURRIES
Pat Chapman Started the Curry Club in 1982. Appears regularly on television and radio and is the author of eighteen books, the latest being *The Thai Restaurant Cookbook*.

BARBECUES AND GRILLS
Brian Turner Chef/patron of Turner's in Knightsbridge and one of Britain's most popular food broadcasters; he appears frequently on *Ready Steady Cook*, *Food and Drink* and many other television programmes.

SUMMER AND WINTER CASSEROLES
Anton Edelmann Maître Chef des Cuisines at the Savoy Hotel, London, and author of six books. He appears regularly on BBC-TV's *Masterchef*.

TRADITIONAL PUDDINGS
Tessa Bramley Chef/patron of the acclaimed Old Vicarage restaurant in Ridgeway, Derbyshire. Author of *The Instinctive Cook*, and a regular presenter on a new Channel 4 daytime series *Here's One I Made Earlier*.

DECORATED CAKES
Jane Asher Author of several cookery books and a novel. She has also appeared in her own television series, *Jane Asher's Christmas* (1995).

FAVOURITE CAKES
Mary Berry One of Britain's leading cookery writers, her numerous books include *Mary Berry's Ultimate Cake Book*. She has made many television and radio appearances and is a regular contributor to cookery magazines.

First published in 1997 by
George Weidenfeld & Nicolson
The Orion Publishing Group
Orion House
5 Upper St Martin's Lane
London WC2H 9EA

British Library Cataloguing-in-Publication data
A catalogue record for this book is available from
the British Library

ISBN 0 297 82281 0

Designed by Lucy Holmes
Edited by Maggie Ramsay
Food styling by Joy Davies
Typeset by Tiger Typeset